Big Thoughts for Little Thinkers

BiG Thoughts for Little Thinkers

Jesus
By Joey Allen

New Leaf Press

First printing: June 2025

Copyright © 2025 by Joey Allen. All rights reserved. No part of this book may be reproduced, copied, broadcast, stored, or shared in any form whatsoever without written permission from the publisher, except in the case of brief quotations in articles and reviews. For information write:

New Leaf Press, P.O. Box 726, Green Forest, AR 72638

New Leaf Press is a division of the New Leaf Publishing Group, LLC.

ISBN: 978-0-89221-773-1

ISBN: 978-1-61458-931-0 (digital)

Library of Congress Control Number: 2025933627

Please consider requesting that a copy of this volume be purchased by your local library system.

Printed in China

Please visit our website for other great titles: www.newleafpress.com.

For information regarding promotional opportunities, please contact the publicity department at pr@nlpg.com.

Illustrations and text by Joey Allen

For Bob and Pam

Pg. 6 image: AXP Photography, unsplash.com

FOREWORD

I have been a fan of the *Big Thoughts for Little Thinkers* books since I first came across them in 2005. What I appreciate about them is the range they cover, reaching all the way up to actual, real theology, and all the way down to straightforward ways of talking, manageable chunks of text, and bright, energetic illustrations. It is exactly the high-to-low range promised in the title; these are indeed big thoughts for little thinkers.

Since first finding the series back then, I have had the chance to meet Joey Allen and even teach him in a graduate theology class (of course he was a great student). Back then I read the books with my own children; now we have the series on the book cart at my church. In fact, my wife (who directs the children's ministry) just told me about one six-year-old girl who runs up to the cart every week asking for these books by name. They are just her size and speed.

This volume, on Jesus, keeps the same high standards and humble format. You will notice it is not just the story of Jesus, but the actual theology of Jesus, from creation to eschatology. It is an ambitious Jesus book for children, and it succeeds wonderfully.

Fred Sanders
Professor of Theology
Torrey Honors College, Biola University

A WORD TO PARENTS AND TEACHERS

Christianity is not primarily a philosophy or a lifestyle, but a relationship with God the Father through Jesus Christ by the Holy Spirit. God's ultimate revelation of Himself is through the carpenter from Nazareth, Jesus, the incarnate Son of God (Hebrews 1:2). Jesus is "the radiance of the glory of God and the exact imprint of His nature, and He upholds the universe by the word of His power. After making purification for sins, He sat down at the right hand of the Majesty on high" (Hebrews 1:3). Jesus is superior to angels, prophets, and priests. Central to historic Christianity is the confession that Jesus mysteriously unites in one person the divine and human natures. Being divine, Jesus can forgive sins, and being human, He can serve as humankind's representative.

I wrote this book to help children encounter the Jesus revealed in Scripture. Jesus is endlessly fascinating. In His character, Jesus displays qualities that normally do not go together. The more we study Jesus, the more we are struck by what Jonathan Edwards calls "the admirable conjunction of diverse excellencies in Jesus Christ." The same Jesus who terrified demons made children feel safe in His arms. He who cleansed the temple with righteous indignation described Himself as "gentle and lowly in heart" (Matthew 11:29). The Great High Priest became the final sacrifice for sins. The Author of Life laid down His life and was raised back to life to put an end to death. The combination of joy and sorrow, strength and meekness, righteousness and grace that Jesus unites in perfect proportion inspires a response of worship. May this book help you introduce the children in your life to Jesus—the incomparable, the indescribable, the Savior and the Sovereign, the Lion and the Lamb, the Alpha and the Omega.

Joey Allen
Chair of Missions and Evangelism, Midwestern Theological Seminary

Hi! My name is Theo. I want you to know and love Jesus because He already loves you. Jesus is more wonderful than I can explain.

John 3:16; 21:25; 1 John 4:10

Jesus is the most important person in history. People all over the world respect Him. Even people who follow different religions think Jesus was a holy man, a wise teacher, or a prophet. People who don't believe in God at all say Jesus was a good example.

Isaiah 45:23; Philippians 2:9

But Christians know that Jesus was much more than a good example, prophet, teacher, or holy man. Christians worship Jesus because He is God.

Matthew 28:9; John 9:37-38; 20:28

We believe in only one true God. God has always been three persons: the Father, the Son, and the Holy Spirit. Jesus is the Son of God who became human.

Luke 1:35, 3:22; John 1:1-2, 14, 18; Romans 5:1-2, 5; 2 Corinthians 13:14; Titus 3:5-6

God created the world through His Son to show His power and love. God made a good and beautiful world. God created humans in His image to rule over His world.

*Genesis 1:26, 28, 31;
Psalm 19:1-6; John 1:3;
Romans 1:20;
Colossians 1:15-17;
Hebrews 1:3*

God's enemy, Satan, tempted the first humans, Adam and Eve. Sadly, they did not trust God, and they disobeyed Him. Disobedience is called "sin." Sin caused a separation between God and humans because God is holy, and we are not.

Genesis 3:1-24; Isaiah 59:2; Romans 3:23; 6:23

The world is still beautiful and good, but because of sin, it has become mixed with selfishness, danger, sickness, and death.

Genesis 1:31; 3:17-19; Romans 5:12; 8:19-22

God promised to send a Savior to destroy Satan, put an end to sin, and make everything right again. Throughout the story of the Bible, God's people eagerly waited for the Savior to come.

Genesis 3:15;
Isaiah 9:6-7

At just the right time, God the Father sent His Son to be the Savior of the world. His name is Jesus, which means "God saves." Jesus is the perfect image of God.

Romans 5:6; Galatians 4:4; Colossians 2:9; Hebrews 1:3; 1 John 4:14

God chose a young woman named Mary to be Jesus' mother. Jesus' birth was a miracle by the Holy Spirit. Every Christmas, we celebrate the birth of Jesus, the Son of God.

Isaiah 7:14; Matthew 1:21-23; Luke 1:26-28, 35

Jesus lived a perfect life. As He grew up, He was always obedient, and He pleased His heavenly Father.

Luke 2:51-52; John 5:19; Hebrews 5:8

When Jesus was about 30 years old, John the Baptist told everyone that Jesus was the Savior of the world. When John baptized Jesus, God the Father spoke from Heaven. He said, "This is My beloved Son." The Holy Spirit came on Jesus in the form of a dove.

Matthew 3:16-17; Luke 3:21-22; John 1:29-34

Then, Jesus went into the wilderness. Satan tempted Jesus, but Jesus trusted His heavenly Father's words and did not sin.

Matthew 4:1; Hebrews 4:15

Jesus began teaching people about God's Kingdom. Jesus taught His followers how to talk to God as their heavenly Father. He told them how to live in a way that pleases God.

Matthew 5:1-10; 6:5-15, 33; 9:35; Mark 4:1-2; Luke 11:1-4; John 14:21-23

Jesus did many miracles. He showed His power over nature when He stopped a thunderstorm and walked on water. He fed more than 5,000 people with just two fish and five pieces of bread. Jesus' miracles reveal how wonderful life will be in His Kingdom.

Matthew 14:13-27;
Mark 6:30-44; 7:31-37;
Luke 8:25;
John 6:1-21, 9:1-7

Jesus showed His power over disease when He healed people who were blind, deaf, and disabled. Jesus showed His power over demons by ordering them to leave. Jesus even showed His power over death by raising dead people back to life.

Matthew 12:22; 15:28; 17:18;
Mark 2:2-12; 5:41-42; Luke 7:11-17; John 11:38-43

Jesus gave special attention to people who others thought were worthless. Jesus spent time with poor people, sick people, and unloved people. Jesus was very kind to babies and children.

Matthew 18:2-10; 19:13-15; Mark 10:13-16; Luke 5:29-32

Jesus is wonderful in every way. He is holy and merciful, wise and joyful, strong and gentle, just and loving, pure and caring. He is the King of kings, but He became human and washed the feet of His disciples.

Exodus 34:6-7; Isaiah 9:6; Matthew 11:28-30; John 13:1-17; Revelation 19:16

The leaders of the world did not believe in Jesus. They were afraid they would lose their power if people followed Jesus. They hated Jesus because they did not believe He was the Son of God.

John 1:11-12; 8:58-59; 11:48

Jesus never did anything wrong, but the leaders of the people made up lies about Jesus and wanted to kill Him. Soldiers made fun of Jesus, beat Him, and then nailed Him to the Cross.

Luke 23:4, 11-15, 20-26, 33;
John 19: 16-18

When Jesus died on the Cross, He took the punishment for our sins. Because Jesus is fully God and fully human, He could die for you and me.

Philippians 2:6-8;
1 John 2:2;
Hebrews 7:24-25
I Peter 2:24

Jesus died and then rose again to rescue us from sin, death, and Satan. Everyone who trusts in Jesus receives forgiveness for sins, becomes a child of God, and has a home in Heaven.

*Ephesians 1:7;
Colossians 1:13–14;
John 1:12; 14:6;
Hebrews 11:6*

After Jesus came back to life, He appeared to over 500 people. He showed His followers where the nails had been in His hands and feet. The story of Jesus is not a fairytale or legend. It *really* happened.

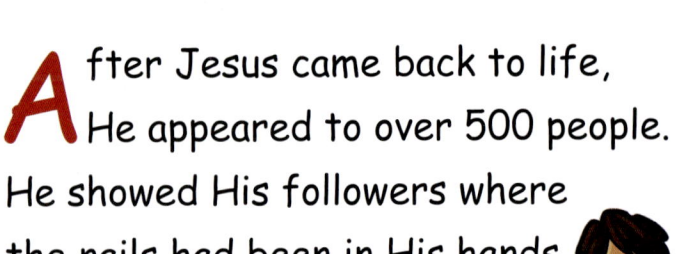

John 20:27-29; 1 Corinthians 15:6; Acts 1:1-5; 1 John 1:1

After 40 days, Jesus rose up to Heaven. Jesus is now in Heaven, preparing a place for us to be with Him.

*John 14:3;
Acts 1:3;
Romans 8:34*

Ten days after Jesus went to Heaven, He sent the Holy Spirit to live in the hearts of all who trust in Him. The Holy Spirit shows us our sins, reminds us of what Jesus taught, comforts us, and helps us obey God and love other people.

John 14:26; 15:26; 16:8; Acts 2:1-4, 17-18; Ephesians 1:13; 3:14-19

One day, Jesus will come back to set up His Kingdom and make Heaven on Earth. There will be no more sin, sadness, sickness, or death in His Kingdom. Everyone who trusts in Jesus will be with Him forever.

John 17:24;
1Thessalonians 4:17;
Revelation 7:16-17;
11:15; 21:4

While we wait for Jesus to return, we should tell others all over the world how wonderful He is and what He has done for us!

John 20:21;
Matthew 28:18-20;
Acts 1:8;
2 Timothy 4:5

Big Thoughts for Little Thinkers